S0-AYX-078

Embrace

To Floyd —

Embrace

poems by

Risa Kaparo

*With all my love
and gratitude

Risa
3/24/02*

Scarlet Tanager
BOOKS

Copyright © 2002 by Risa Kaparo
All rights reserved
Printed in the United States of America

Cover design: Risa Kaparo and David Boulton
Text Design: Andrea DuFlon, Berkeley, CA
Composition: Archetype Typography, Berkeley, CA
Photos: Ellen Wolfe
Cover print inspired by "Woman with Birds," a painting by Shin Tao Kuang

Published by Scarlet Tanager Books
P.O. Box 20906
Oakland, CA 94620
www.scarlettanager.com

Library of Congress Cataloging-in-Publication Data
Kaparo, Risa
    Embrace : poems / by Risa Kaparo.
        p. cm.
    ISBN 0-9670224-6-0 (alk. paper)
    I. Title.
    PS3611.A77 E43 2002
    811'.6—dc21

                                                2002000074

Acknowledgments

Though space does not permit me to thank everyone whose friendship, inspiration and support has made this book possible, they fill the space in my heart always.

I am grateful to the following poets: Richard Garcia—for his inspiration in those days we spent writing together on my deck. Gail Shafarman—for her friendship and feedback in the early phase of compiling this collection. Richard Silberg—for his generous encouragement and mentoring. Members of my writing group, *The Sands of Tam,* especially Dawn Kawahara and Francis Frazier for their support.

To musicians, Gary David, Kimba Arem and Jorge Ayala, a warm mahalo for their guidance and participation on the CD recording of *Embrace.*

I want to thank Lucy Day for all her kind attention in seeing this book published.

To artists Nancy Margulies, Andrea Duflon, Ralph Adamson and most especially David Boulton, my deepest gratitude.

I also wish to thank the editors of the following publications and anthologies in which some of the poems in this collection first appeared, sometimes in different versions:

Arts: "Disappearing Sands," "Night Whispers"

Blue Unicorn: "Deanna's Magic Keys"

ETC., A Review of General Semantics: "Waste," "Awake"

East Bay Journal: "Home," "The Cracked Bowl"

ForPoetry.com: "Night Currents," "In Winter"

Manzanita Quarterly Literary Review: "Salad," "The Legacy"

More E-Prime: To Be or Not II (International Society of General Semantics): "Waste"

Poetry Flash: "Sorting Eggs," first published under the title "Letter To Myself"

PoetryMagazine.com: "Salad," "Shorn," "The Legacy," "Blades"

Psychological Perspectives: "Exequy of Sand," "Night Currents"

RedRiverReview.com: "Before"

SugarMule.com: "The Cracked Bowl"

The Dallas Review: "Portrait of Two," first published as "Midnight," "Six O'clock," "Sundown," and "Ten O'clock"

The Phoenix Journal: "After the Firestorm"

Wellness Associates Journal: "Thirty-sixth Return," "Almost Four"

Writing For Our Lives: "Elegy for Father," "Encounter"

for Deanna
for the children

Contents

Initiations by Fire

The Mouths of Women in Love

To Be Lifted Like a Child to a Kiss

The theme of this collection was inspired by an old fairy tale in which a handless maiden comes upon a drowning child. Despite the impossibility, she reaches to save the child and hands miraculously appear.

We all experience such moments—where impossibility is overcome by necessity—where we are challenged to extend beyond our sense of limitation—where we have no choice but to embrace the gift of what is.

Awake

like children who've slept with their bellies empty
rush into the streets
hungry to eat the morning
like rock quickens with tendrils of light

I've walked with the sun until night fell
forgetful of the reason of hours
still the road rears its head
slithers like a snake beneath my feet
midnight clings to my breast
coils its blue flesh about me
now flames of stars
lick my body
flames like mouths of women
in love

I am nothing
embrace me
even nothing can not last

This Rare and Perilous Life

Shorn

You were weary.
Two colicky babies then the unwanted pregnancies
and one you couldn't abort.
Your hand grasping her skinny wrist
tugging arm from shoulder.
She would not budge from that sidewalk.
A single act of defiance
on Laurelton Boulevard
that chilly Saturday morning.
Do with her what you will.
She will not
give in.

Moments before
while you spoke through the mirror
she disappeared from herself.
Even the barber's leathery hand,
prying her tiny chin from chest
so you could admire such a cute pixie,
was washed clean by tears.

The floor a graveyard:
trampled manes and tails,
wild beasts crushed underfoot.

Having prevailed
you lit your cigarette
leaning against the barbershop window
to rest sore feet before the long walk
even in your comfortable shoes.
The scolding, the razored flecks of hair,
for her own good.

Other mothers scurried by
yanking the arm leash of children.

Your threats—giving her something to really cry about—
couldn't dam her tears.
They washed over bands of your Indian burns,
bracelets of defiance replacing a kindergartner's pride.

Until bangs curtained her eyes
weeks went by.
Not showers nor sleep nor school
not even the shame-weakened muscles of her neck
parted that pixie head from brother's football helmet.

Mother, I am she
that wild beast
caught and captive.
Never attempting escape.
Even when the cage opens.
No longer believing
freedom.

Dancing Lessons

Inside her bubble
time is unmoored,
impulsive,
sap seeping through her tissues.
The little girl is a log languidly spinning
a sudden updraft
        birds lifting in flight
or trembling
        the way an eye opens when injured.

The little girl, in stillness
sensing how music finds her,
plays her, moonlight on water.
Movement imperceptible at first
slowly undulates.
Her skin a membrane of light
her fingers—antennas
tuned to different wavelengths.
The waves unfurling to rivulets
the rivulets unraveling her arms.
She is a fluid landscape pouring
into the hands of an invisible surveyor,
elbow and knee sharing a timorous discourse
then away
glancing back from distance
behaving like suitors sending love notes
traffic in the bloodstream.

Her teacher honors her dancing
the little girl's native intuitions
how she feels what she feels
beyond memory, beyond imagination.

The little girl fought for this privilege.
Fought a father who terrified her
                used her for entertainment.
Fought this once
for sovereignty.
Staking the small world she choreographed
for sovereignty.

Had to
and won.

Dogs

She was late returning from her dancing lesson
nearly 6:00 when he found her.
Scrapes and bruises:
her bony knees, hips, thighs
the tiny buds of her breasts
her face
the prepubescent glow
washed from her cheeks
a few clumps of her hair—
long black-walnut strands torn from her scalp
her short fingernails dirty with their skin
her dark skin white with fear
her teeth red with the blood of one
her shins glittering with asphalt
her clothes in tatters

Her older brother, a husky thirteen
dragging her to the station
The girl squatting on the corner of Wetherole and Woodhaven
pulling against his grip
pulling away from her own body
pleading, *No, I can't*
Please . . . don't make me . . . please, no police

She knew one of them
an older brother of the boy next door
the one who showed off at recess

These were ordinary boys
acting the way dogs
even the most obedient
behave when they pack

The girl and her brother never speak of it again
making elaborate detours and excuses
she never again walks that way alone

There is a place in the bullring where the bull feels safe. If he can reach this place, he stops running and can gather his full strength. He is no longer afraid. From the point of view of his opponent, he becomes dangerous. This place in the ring is different for every bull. It is the job of the matador to be aware of this, to know where sanctuary lies for each and every bull, to be sure that the bull does not occupy his place of wholeness.

In bullfighting the safe place is called the querencia.

Rachel Naomi Remen

Querencia

This three-year-old has no words
for alone
refusing ordinary language
for the privacy of baby talk

If only she had won her sister's heart
they might have slept beside one another
the little one nuzzling in for protection
but at seven her sister lay in her own bed of shame

Now the little one sits vigil
alone
fighting sleep
and voices incessant within
the layered darkness
shadows dancing on doors
She sits bolt upright in bed
the strained alertness
her only defense

All of them men,
the one she could not believe
was her father, his den of witches
stealing the sleeping body
while her soul wandered
inside the walls

a ghost
searching for that safe place

She once hurt so bad
she took the risk
showed her mother
the flames in her vulva
blood trickling from the darkness within,
afraid she'd spill her insides
That's when the holding began
Paralysis
the relentless vigilance

Tied up by her own fears
Mother betrays the secret
Father decides to treat the girl
himself
That was the last
she revealed to anyone

Thirty years
the little one remains in hiding
like the clay-caked mounds of flesh,
children who buried themselves neck deep
surviving the last big war
venturing into the forest by night
to chew wild grubs
when everything stands invisible

Last night I found her amidst muffled cries
I will hold her thin bones against my ample flesh
till the quivering subsides

Some who survived the camps
remember those who made rounds
to console others, offering their last crumb of bread

What will you do with the rare and perilous life
given you?

Dawn begins in the bones

Shiva

We slid the two blocks separating school from home, gray slush mounted at curbs, rainbow slicks on puddled roads. You always beat me.

Racing up six flights of concrete stairs, blue doors swirling. It must have been your long legs that matched fingers I always envied. Even toes grew delicate and shapely on you. And those Persian lashes, thick and darker than mine, far more exotic.

Adding our shoes to the bumpy lineup carpeting the hallway to your door, you'd jump the only piece of furniture in the front room and fetch the can of honey. I watched you paint a thick shellac over white buttered bread for the better part of a month before trying it. At home, honey meant sore throats. You couldn't pay me to swallow.

We'd drip a sticky trail into the room staggered with cots, all five facing different directions. The beds moved so often I wondered how you knew which was yours until I noticed the nightgown tucked halfway beneath a pillow, too small to fit the others.

It seemed strange to me—your father and Hassan in one room, your mother with you and your sisters. I tried to feel what it would be like to share a room with my mother. I couldn't. But, I remember wishing I had your mother. Eyes so kind. I never cried until she gazed at me. Held in her glance everything fell away: all that tough indifference.

I didn't know whether to believe you. But I loved the stories. And those drawings so flushed with color I didn't dare to copy. Views off the east wing of your country mansion, the sculptured gardens, servants and artists and scholars. You who kept all your belongings—a rolled up pad of paper, broken crayons, a ball and twelve jacks—inside one shoe box. I couldn't imagine how it ended—the story you didn't tell. Or what it felt like to lose your past and not your pride.

I always wondered what happened, Shiva. I looked for a note around the empty apartment the day you disappeared like the oil we poured back into bottles after frying cold spaghetti and thought no one ever knew.

10

Before
for Andy

I did not remember
spooning on the bed, watching Hepburn and Taylor
on the four-inch Sony that I had begged almost a year for.
And pretending not to notice
when your hand came to rest on my waist,
the studied screen forging my composure.

I did not remember
until the feeling lapped against my mourning
the delicate lace of your breath on my neck
our muscles
sweetening.
How we laid so still
belonging.

And just beneath the skin—two horses
carving up the hillside, the wild
endurance, the rearing up, longing turning
upon itself, the dread of time.

They told me your spine snapped even before you hit the water
before the earth had ever rushed through your fingers
before I could offer myself to you.

The Legacy

The Legacy
for Bubba & Zaida

The smell of rotting leaves and white ginger
rose pungent off rain-damp streets
past mown fields edged purple with bougainvillea
and seeing a hyacinth
red as the lipstick that stained my cheeks when last I saw her
I found my dead Bubba again
sitting on a wooden bench threading three purls
and one knit into a band of blue

Before they removed the tumor from her brain
Bubba baked a wooden barrel full of rougalah
just in case
She flew to California a week later
to greet her newest grandchild
before the surgeons could graft a plate to her skull
a flap of skin separating brain from sky
a gypsy scarf, red and gold, widening
and narrowing to her cerebral pulse

Years later
I visited her in the hospital again, eyes glazed
from electric shock, drugs
her dressing gown drooping off one shoulder
back exposed
her wit and humor, that unmistakable belly laugh
irrepressible

No one knew why, but in the kitchen
while borscht and simmering onions sweetened the scent of liver
rising off the stove, Bubba chased Zaida around the table
the chopping knife clenched in her knotted fist

I walked past the drooling figures that lined the visiting room
to tell Bubba I got engaged. *Don't give yourself away*
She whispered when we were finally alone
When you're my age and can't spread your legs anymore
they treat you like shit

Three husbands later, I took Bubba's name
Not when she died, but years after
breaking bread with my Aunties
I heard how Bubba was sent to the city at twelve
one less mouth to feed
in the war torn Romania that killed her father

While her mother tilled the farm
working as a blacksmith
to shelter four other children
Bubba served as cook and chambermaid
a well-to-do uncle having his way with her

That night, for the first time, I heard Bubba's name
not the name stamped on her papers at Ellis Island
her ebony eyes buoyant with hope
all that mattered folded neatly in one suitcase

Not Weiner, Itzkiwitz, or Zuckor
nor any other name
Bubba's mother stole
like a crust of bread to keep her boys alive
each time the draft found them
She was born to the name
Kaparo, from the Hebrew *to forgive*
a sacrifice for atonement

Soon after I took Bubba's name
fire purged what remained of my life
the framed relief of a shtetel kitchen
she sent to me when they closed the house in Flatbush
where she raised five children with broken English
where I whiled many a childhood hour
the package filled with rougalah
Ash to ash

All that I have of my Bubba
I give to my daughter
her name
her history

Waste

She probably had no family or will—a ward of the state—
one of the nameless. Still she arrived basically intact
except for the feet and head
which went to the dental and podiatry schools.
Someone helps me lift her from the shelf and
roll her out of the refrigerated room.
I lean in for the first cut but withdraw my scalpel
having neglected to secure the wheels.
I stop. Removing the mask
from my mouth and nose, I touch
one palm of the latex glove against the other
for a moment close my eyes—
needing to find some way
of respect.

Taking a deep breath, I press the blade through several layers
of skin and subcutaneous tissue, cutting along the sternum.
Then since nothing else will do
I break into her flesh with my fingernails,
peel back the sheaths
of fascia. Her left breast
falls into my hand
still embedded in its husk of skin.

As the cadaver warms, the air grows heavier with formaldehyde.
I cut into the abdomen and feel nausea.
The stench of adipose tissue—reeking more lurid
than muscle, skin, bone.
I look around the stainless steel and formica room
wishing for plants that metabolize the chemical.
I Imagine the time when earth lay covered in green, the plants
smothering in their own waste. This
before the advent
of a new class   *mammalia*
that could live off that oxygen.

In winter when the earth lay creatively fallow, Rudolf Steiner
blended manure with rotting compost,
potentialized the mixture
homeopathically
and buried it in antlers
to draw power from the stars.

He never used human feces
to fertilize soil for our consumption
because he felt we've already abstracted
what we need from our food
the way a cow takes substance to fatten on
and leaves the stuff of human intelligence untouched.
I think of our waste,
the feces and urine, carbon dioxide
garbage and chemicals
and that other waste—
the meaning
I wonder what we leave behind that could nourish another
or whether we could learn to live
                              off our own waste.
I think of my mother's dying still to come.

I cut through the sternum with a power saw, dig my hands
between the ribs and pull as hard as I can.
Membranes tear into strands that gleam like water webs.
And the colors—teals and lilacs, even after the formaldehyde
or maybe because of it, I do not know.
I lift the fine lace of her lungs on the tips of two fingers and blow
gently, the way children do with dandelions. I watch them
float on my breath.

Confrontation

What is it you want to hear me say?
That I beat you?
Is that it?
I am your father; I had the right
to discipline. Then what?
What? That I tied you up?
Locked you in the closet?
Stop this now!

I didn't do it.
You must believe me.
How do you know?
Could you see the face?
                  Wasn't it dark?
How could you do this to me? I love you.

Elegy for Father

At first it came just once or twice in the morning
your bowels loosed their undigested load
like the ravaged embankment of a river.
Then only occasionally when you'd lie down
that feeling of suffocation
as though something had lodged in your throat.
You remember Kenya, the white peacock
we saw swallow the hummingbird
whole. The lump, still fluttering
half way down his long neck.
The southern boy you chose.
New Blood.

You spun your web of magic around him
reading plays aloud,
the shadows of characters cast large,
larger than the Empire State Building,
the phallus
enshrined in your penthouse window.
A vampire seducing his consort.

I want to stop you
but it's too late.
Now his twenty-four-year life quivers before me.
Couldn't we be strangers?
I don't want to feel responsible.
Like when I asked
about precautions and you said
you didn't need any. You already have the virus.

"Your daddy was the best thing ever
happened to me."
Even having witnessed your body
wasting, he'd offer his blood again
to assuage your hunger.

I want to tell him you knew all along
but I can't, as though truth
were the real virus.
I never wondered how someone could love
and kill the same person, until you
dragged it home.

Toward the end, his firm grip holding your fingers
steady around pliers. Hands that once honored gold
with their sculpting. Useless.
Those deaths along the way. The way
you shiver beneath blankets, inconsolable.
The coldness of the grave
before the grave.
I rushed across town from the apartment.
Eager to wash away your private world
I scraped the sand
and cold gray froth against my skin.
The red carnation
I tore from your grave slapped against the shore.
The sea would not receive it.

Strange, how much it meant
to learn you knew of the child I carry.

The Impossibility of Eros

Sorting Eggs

I spent the night sorting eggs
giving just the time each required to be cared for properly,
placed so that not one would break.
Crimson streaks scratch an ascending sky—
feeling as though someone ripped me from a torrent,
laid me out to dry on this place of refuge.

Last night, bending over to kiss you
you parting your lips to me
I cautiously responded
my tongue circling the shallow of your mouth.
Then you grasped my head
and my heart beat fast.
Suddenly it wasn't excitement
but fear.
Your callused fingers
a pumice against such thin folds of flesh
and still you rubbed hard though I've told you
many times.
When you pushed me down on your sex
my eyes opened to my father
hovering above my body
a plane poised for landing.

I drifted into the walls
reassuring myself like a mantra against expectancy:

If you love me you will do anything.
It will soon be over.

Want what I want.
In the morning it will be as if nothing happened.

Then you rolled over
never touched me again. Not
an arm around my waist or shoulder.
Not a word.

Night Currents

She leans over a porcelain bowl,
rinses her face with lavender.
Water streaks down her cheeks
as she answers the phone.
His voice searches the space around her.
He feels her there alone. His voice
she tastes without swallowing,
lets it linger in her mouth like fine curry,
the spices—waves riding her tongue:
cardamom, coriander, cumin, clove.

She knows he has dreamt of her again.
She feels that remorse he carries on such nights
when he comes to her
like a tribesman to confess
dreaming harm to a companion.

He comes to her as one to a lake,
kneels,
cups her in his palms,
feels her spill upon his crown,
his forehead.
Drawing fingers to his mouth
he drinks of her.

He awakens
finds himself immersed
completely.
He leaves
as if it were a sin
to love water.

In Winter

He felt suspicious of this woman,
of the yes she lived unambivalently,
of the distance she traveled that he
had never known.

How could he know of the years in which that yes
grew within her
the way a bamboo leaf bends under the
weight of mounting snow?
How could he trust it? Seeing only
the sudden slide of snow to the ground,
and the leaf not stirred.

Cold Fusion

He cannot help loving the face he sees in hers
she cannot see
they fight
he wants to open but resents
he cannot help loving her
she is family, even if he feels alone
sometimes
these times
he cannot stand her

Tracks

Last night
you entered bed from the far end
rolled onto your left side
without a kiss goodnight.

I lay still for a moment
sensing pain in your body, sensing mine, then
gently wrapped myself around your spine.
When you moved out of my caress
my heart swooped low
as though the wind had lost its substance.
And from the canyon's depths
I saw my mother
coming from the kitchen where even aching
with tiredness, she spoke so kindly
on the phone with friends.
But alone in darkness
her touch disgusted me.
She grabbed, twisted and pinched
burning into my skin
the tracks of her fingernails.

And you, sweet love,
how I wanted to hold and be held
as in those nights of childhood longing
and just moments before
your gentleness on the phone with others.
I lay at your side
vacant of you,
the child's soul roaming ghostlike
through walls, as if love were the only wind
to lift the heart.

Beyond Normal Marital Sadism

I claw myself awake
call you out
knead knuckles to ribs
pull sword from sheath
expose us

allow the fierce paradox
eros and anger
to break in, take hold
cleave us
stem to crown
withhold nothing

fear not my passion
rise to me   play
be half the man fighting
that you otherwise are
and we would least dread
landing in shadow

come alive
teethe my flesh blue and shining
draw chi through your kidneys
fuck me

Retreat

The calico scurries beneath the porch
before the river cat's approach.
She has grown too nervous to eat.

With the first glimmer of morning
man of my heart rushes
from my bed
to rescue his privacy.
Before I awake

he has returned the solitude
I have not yet lost.

She

Your name, what remained with me
through the cycles of blood and tides
a ribbon wound about my waist
rosaries of dream—
the child we imagined each time
the moon rounded.
She waits in the foyer
then disappears.
And though I carried
all vertebrate imagination
in my womb,
it was not enough.

Blades

Through the blurred tabla and flight of ragas
seeing without sense the hundred faces
scattered over tables, waiters darting in pandemonium
like birds scavenging the streets of Calcutta.
A little girl nearby, hair of winter weed and wet
charcoal eyes, her glance piercing through frantic voices.
She watches the magic of my pen drawing lines that speak.

Could she know my loneliness and tonight's vacant sleep?
The sitar's moan, my own intoxication.
It is barren between two worlds.   I could almost prefer
a betrayer's touch,
his hands pinning down my arms, unloosing
his cum between swollen lips.   I would almost prefer this

abused awakening.
More than once, you held the knife like an oracle
pointing the way.
Now it is I who must drive the blade
and your old heart beating.
It does not cease easily,
this resilient blood habit.

How the ritual goodbye took comfort
from my never leaving. Always you would wake
to me beneath the fine limbed maple, and beside me
slip into the dream of our forgetting.
Now I must enter a different solitude.
I must walk on that dirt road
past all the times I have left before—
and not
return.

Initiations by Fire

The Cracked Bowl

Running the crystal edge with a leather wand
stirred sweet tones into the wind
the sounding bowl
all that remained intact when we arrived
the ash, some embers still aglow
two days after the fire, the bowl surviving
heat over two thousand degrees
the distance off the mantel
and the crumbling second story floor, to land
whole
amidst the rubble

I lifted it like the Zen gardener
who after long afternoons
sitting in a quarry, tenderly
rolling his tobacco into rounds
inhales
finally rises—

touches the edge with one finger
the rock splits open, unveils
a millennium, the history of this
place, story of creation

the crystal bowl opens in my hands
the way lips part to form sound
the last sound a crack—
how it waited through the forging of fire
the fall, burial beneath ruins
the fracture
hidden until that moment
my two hands lifted it, awed

the touch unraveling matter
through the veins of stories unknown:
rock
woman
bowl

On October 20, 1991 a firestorm ripped through the
Oakland hills. Nearly 3,500 families lost their homes.
Twenty-five people lost their lives.

Home

He drives fast and steady.
Except around curves his right arm remains
with me, returns the pressure of my palm
with his muscle and flesh.   We have never
touched like this before.
The hills of my home already in flames,
we arrive at a friend's cabin
and he asks,
Could I stay with you tonight?

Barely morning, still awake
remembering a gift, the pregnant figure
of a hermaphrodite god, phallus erect.   The years I looked
up from my bed into its spread wings
imagining a man with breasts and womb
who would offer his substance
freely.

The hillside still burns.
Ribbons of memory unfurl as smoke,
carried by wind into the nostrils of dreamers
everywhere.   Nothing is lost.
The shtetel kitchen carved into a wooden frame
each dish, smaller than a dime, decorated with flowers.
The hours I played inside its magic, standing on a chair
near Bubba's table—dreaming the dreamer.
The Romanian countryside, a postcard-size rendering
framed by the doorway.
The onions and garlic chopped into charred eggplant.

His hand leaves my side. The echo of his touch.
My senses streaming.
All that has ever been is at once alive.
The gold posts that first pierced my ears
in days when my father still called me Gingging.
Mother's crocheted tablecloths, the depression glass.
Those cherubs Zaida hung where his girl-children slept.

The Japanese ink scroll—a tiny boat, the faint
silhouette of a mountain,
the undifferentiated wholeness
they point to.
The ash.

The squirrels.   I close my eyes.
Did their fur ignite when the plum trees caught
and the limbs cracked off that burly crone of a pine?
Surely she bore witness till the last.
No more rustling of wind.
His skin whispers:
I am here.

Ride your horse on the edge of the sword
Hide yourself in the center of the flame
Blossoms of the fruit tree bloom in the fire
The sun rises in the evening
                    Zen koan

Overtones

I

As the fire storms up the hillside
we weave our way through the cacophony
people pouring into the streets
A woman carrying a child in one arm,
flung over the other shoulder
some precious things wrapped in a tablecloth
A man shouts after his wife as she stoops to tie her son's laces
The screeching brakes, overtones to the cries
Your fingers wrap firmly around mine—
so small
in your hand
and running
the pavement hurled underfoot, pavement
burning through our shoes
and running
into the center of the flame
There, sheltered by the fire
we stop
see into the eyes of the other
find ourselves
in the new life
The sun rises in the evening

II

Blossoms of the fruit tree born of the fire
lie strewn about the ground
Living by your side
already a horse running the edge of a blade
Having placed my heart
most delicate
in your hands
I slide down the cracks between fingers

wake to the free fall
long tendrils
floating

After the Firestorm

I found him wandering along my street
I had to touch him
the old man
I reached for his left arm, dangling in the shirt sleeve
folds of air
loose flesh along a narrow bone

The touch   tentative at first
like a pat one gives to reassure a child
suddenly fell through our skin
as through nothing

Later I saw his photograph in the paper
He had roamed the streets for three days
when officials picked him up

As they pushed him behind the barricades
firefighters assured him:
Everyone has been evacuated

He got past them just before morning
Nothing remained of his wife
nothing you could distinguish
from remains of buildings, trees, animals
He said she couldn't walk

For a moment his eyes
closed as I drew away
dark rings rounding the moon

Behind us, a lone chimney
that stood for everything lost
In my hand, a tiny circle of jade
a heart of silver fired to a crust of ash

Exequy of Sand

Sycamore leaves and that early morning light,
silhouettes dispersed upon the ceiling,
her arm, its weight settled evenly across his chest
as though a night wind had strewn a mound of sand
   along the ridge.
He did not feel it.

The room was carefully arranged,
each book, each photograph resting just where it belonged
but she
had no image to recover, nor anyone
on whom she could depend,
not even herself.

Desires, those winged creatures,
great birds of imagination
so awkward on the ground.
The necessity—as if her body required devastation by fire
to set off those latent seeds of a clandestine journey,
having refused the landscape of ordinary concerns.

Somehow the cells seemed to know.
There was only to receive the kiss,
the tide having traveled great distance to land on her shores.
So long since the last of such tides visited
it was a different body,
none of whose cells remain.

She takes up the burden of living
like a rock in hand—
feels its weight sink
through muscle and bone, one order of present
enfolding another.
She calls upon gravity
to deliver her.

Black Waters

The road is red and ends in forests of island pine.
Winter solstice.
Under Green Mountain
a path goes west, tunnel of dark waters
warmed by fire that melts rock.
After two nights' fitful dreaming
I walk stiffly,
vast ocean of blackness to my right,
to my left
stringy silhouettes of ohias
black against black.
Even the plumeria are black tonight,
petals strewn across the footpath.
There are no snakes here.

I stand before the wooden lighthouse
where Pele's fierce flood of passion parted
just enough to encircle the beacon
rushing red-gold to the sea.
I have come in obedience to a call that I cannot answer;
still I come like the woman with no hands
to save a drowning child.

I dive into blackness,
I cannot do otherwise.
Waves undulate from my spine, rippling
far beyond my senses.
Below me there is black.
Above me
        black.
No longer can I tell direction.

The shrill pleading of an old woman—
her voice presses against my skin—forms my shape with sound—
still I swim on . . .
When I hear the entreaties of a dying man
my heart chokes on the sudden viscosity of my blood.
I am flushed to the surface. The tail swipe of a white shark.
Death does not take its offering.

I plunge forward only on strong currents,
between waves
                    resting.
It is asleep on black sand that she finds me,
carries me home.

The Mouths of Women in Love

Departures

Long after you caught my attention,
taking up my reveries as if they had always and only
    belonged to you,
weeks had stretched since I first rushed my words
    over the ends of yours
so eager to ride the waves of your mouth and still
I did not know.

Not until walking at the station. You stopped
and greeting a stranger carrying *The Denial of Death*
said you didn't want to leave.
We talked about going for coffee but never
moved off that platform,
staggering a few steps from one another
when we could no longer
stand so close and not touch.
I never gave you my affection.
You took it
your grasp unfurling my spine.

In the end, when your lips released
confusion against my cheek, and exhaled
the scent of my hair, that I, too, might taste it,
I had no home to return to anymore.

Portrait of Two

Midnight

I come out from the bathroom
and see you standing in the frayed shirt
you often sleep in, the one that buttons at the neck.
You are looking through my bookshelves
and I stand in the darkened hallway
for a moment of you.
I think when you die,
I will make a paste to wash your bones,
grinding my saliva into rotting thatch.
I will cover them with needles of white pine.
I think of this when I see your legs. I think
bones like these can only be borrowed.
You notice me in the hall and take your turn
in the bathroom,
closing the door as I pass because
it is not time, you think, to share
such secrets.

Six O'clock

Where my hand slides beneath the comforter, the sheet
has already cooled.   From the hall
I see your black hair against the white couch pillow—
the coffee you nurse smells strong.
I lean against the wall forgetting I had to pee
and watch you watch the squirrels
run across the plum trees
to the roof and back again, making a thud
each time they cross.
I have the sense you feel me standing in the doorway
and you do not turn around.

Sundown

I catch a glimpse of you through the window
at the back of the house.   You are studying
fence posts and shaking your head.   Your figure
disappears behind the redwood, and I know the carpenter
will hear from you tomorrow.
You will talk to him about taking pride in one's work,
and he will listen to you
though you do not live here or sign his checks.
It is several minutes before I hear your keys drop
upon the bookcase beside the door.

Ten O'clock

I am lying on my bed
talking with you on the telephone.
We're chatting about our work and I ask
what you have on.
You're wearing jeans
and your gray sweater.   And I hear
your shoes drop, one shoe
squeaking free against the toe of the other
and I imagine it is the left which falls first.
There is a new fullness to your breathing,
I picture you reclined.
I can't decide whether to see you in the front room
or on your bed or
if it matters, but it seems to, so I ask.
You tell me a scented candle burns upon your nightstand
and the rose quartz you are squeezing
grows warmer in your hand.
I tell you my fingers
are wet.

Night Whispers

After our loving loosens the tightness in your back
and your arms form a weightless liquid around my breathing
your voice, through the veils of sleep,
etches into my heart the way
veins of fire cut across a prairie

This blaze,
what daylight cannot translate—
the skin hunger
the remembrance of water

Arguments of Desire

She leaves the moon wading over her left shoulder,
sets it atop ragged waves of green.
Because her lover has flown
into the stilled blue
she enters the secreted place of her ancestors.

On the steps she sheds her cloak,
awakens the lioness from her depths.
Muscles of her legs ripen around fire in the bones.

She climbs upon a star,
spreads her claws toward a yellowing moon,
shreds it into net,
casts it upon the hillside,
hurling the arguments of desire.

From the ridge top
she sees her love return,
grieving.
She cannot come to him like this,
her lion paws
kneading the ground into a hungry firmament.

Her lover sleeps
but does not rest.
His spine writhing through dream
lulls the sky lower,
gathers invisible threads that render the moon
its substance.

Dragon Lover

As bats who hang feet curled in the bowels
of mountains, descend from musky caverns,
I mount the wounded lamplight and sail
the desert on a windless night.

You come to me with the ruby eyes of dragon,
backlit, dive into a seashell of nectars,
drumming the wail of sirens into a sinuous ground.

Soaked in the sweat of invisible horses
we paint the flavor of drunken meadows,
drinking the last blood of dawn.

Disappearing Sands

She has traveled thousands of miles to worship here
to lift you in cupped hands
splash you over the flesh of memory
wet the hollow of her throat with salt sweet mist.
In the alchemy of moon-drenched waters, diaphanous waters,
the woman dressed in garments of the sea
plunges through eddies of liquid opal
dives through the dark manes of gulf-weed
spreading a field of white flowers adrift the waves,
black hair floating
like spider threads in warm primordial tarns.
Black eyes sipping sweet coral from the labyrinth of your voice.
Pearls rise off a hidden landscape
billowing out between thighs.
She presses further,
legs thrusting,
       a convulsion of wings.
It ends in a riot of cyan
at the graves of children drowned in mirrors
bathed beyond the powers of prayer.

To Be Lifted Like a Child to a Kiss

Thirty-Sixth Return

Before you were born
your godmother told me of your coming.
She came again to greet you when
curled into a crest of moon
you rose into the blue ink of my belly
two days after conception.

Sometimes, you look upon the hearthstone of my body,
and I think you remember.
On the thirty-sixth return of the earth's journey around the sun,
from the day of my birth,
we make love that morning.

Your spirit enters the pores of my skin with his touch.
When you come to my womb, my womb
unravels to structureless ground,
a sea without horizon.
All the activities that constitute life,
your body,
form from this covenant.

In the streaming of a cytoplasmic madness
cells multiply.
Then your faint heartbeat, the first kick.
We play. Harnessing pressure from my hands
firm against tailbone and feet—
you surf gravity,
elongating
space between vertebrae.

A circle of women enact your blessing way.
They shower us in barley, salt, moonwater.

May you never want from hunger,
      body or soul.
May you carry the wisdom of earth.
May you always feel our sisterhood.

Then sky turns inside out.
Pressure of milk at my breasts,
pigment migrating to nipples,
we make love that morning.

Muscular yearnings rise like serpents
penetrating the web of nerves along my spine.
A quickening—like fear, but ecstatic, summoning—
hormones cascade, climb through branches of vein.

Braced against the knees of your godmother,
I shed skin
of five thousand years.

                    I am a snake molting, a fish
                    undulating, a wolf
                    howling in short bursts, rising
                        to circle the den.

You plunge forward only on strong currents,
between waves, resting.
For a moment the crown of your head crests
and disappears.
The next tide flushes you to the surface.
She lifts you from the water.
Sound of your voice
breathing air.

Circle the Sun

My daughter turns three tomorrow
Tonight I gather photos of each age
remembering her life

She will circle a candlelight sun
earth in hand
walking once around
for each year of her journey

At birth
cradled in the crook of my arm
her limbs floating effortless
her mouth pressed against a generous mountain

At one
flung between mom and dad
joy rushing her cheeks
laughter innocent as rain

At two
her azure eyes smiling back through the photo
I see the world
transformed
in one generation
the fear lifted as if by wings

Almost Four

Twilight saturates the garden
as the three follow the cats into cat lady's bedroom
taking in the linger of chevre and olives, scent of primrose.
The youngest, almost four, sits
fingers curling copper ringlets
and just-right pressure
against thumb-sweet hard-palette.
Eyes heavy lidded, gazing—
spectacle of grown women playing dress-up—
silhouettes of contour beneath flow of fabric,
cascading colors, skin exuding a lush, moist fragrance.
The easy gift they are to each other.
Her lids struggle against gravity.

Almost four tastes
being woman,
whole body, tone on tone,
mystery and nuance—
lavish as the first strawberry ripened in her garden.

Grace of leisure to share such firsts:
tingle of silk floating across her skin,
the rustle when she walks,
hem of scarf fanning her toes,
tied just below her navel, pleasure of fullness.
Standing before the tall mirror
she studies form without image.
Her presence extends into the reflection, filling it with poise.
Wrap of our glance she wears without coyness or seduction,
sheltered by the marvel.

Almost four knows what she wants.
She has not practiced the tacit *irrelevation* of desire—
I, her mother, blushing at honesty—

almost four rejecting one top after another. *Too big, no . . .*
not this one,
her toes pushing her eyes over the ledge of the cat lady's
lingerie drawer.
Ah—the just-rightness
Egyptian cotton, immediately apprehendable—
princess, ringlets, camisole, sarong.
Iridescent heart swinging wildly.
Grace of passage, almost four.

First Communion

I am brought here by my daughter
found waist deep in mud today
thrown off the little bridge which separates
kindergartners from tadpoles,
the youngest deciding he would not succumb
to her—all 49 inches, 49 pounds of muscular yearning
decorated with ribbons and curls, lipstick
(when she can get away with it), tattoos and glitter.

We spend our togetherness on walks
she, her father, I
finding our footing through sand, cane, red dirt
walking this island, step by step,
under new moons and full.

These walks—our tryst with owl,
my daughter's 'Aumakua
messenger of secret omens
whose swift movements and keen sight link the dark
unseen world to the world of light.

Gracing our first walk through this jungle of naupaka
and hila-hila grass, the owl perched low upon a stump,
gazed unblinkingly into those wild eyes
unmasking the soul of the world to my daughter's naked
perception.

Here ironwoods stream like hair along the headlands
forming pockets of windbreak when the trades are strong.
Sheltered within I tell my daughter
the legend of naupaka
story of lovers torn asunder
searching lush foliage
to witness how plants change with grief,

the act of feeling transforming the world. Half flowers
on naupaka o kai, half flowers on naupaka o uka,
sea and mountain naupaka,
never connecting.

She asks me when they will meet again
as though she remembers
longing
beckoning the beloved

Then the sudden flutter of wings overhead

Deanna's Magic Keys

My daughter jiggles a cyber pet
she sneaks out for the walk. She says

Mom, do you know what I can do with these keys?

Well, the first key opens anything you want—like a store or a house.

And the second key takes you there, butcept
you don't have to take an airplane or car.
Just turn the key and you're at Disneyland.   Or Africa.
Anywhere you want without having to get there.

You mean it eliminates space?
Do you jump like Alice through the rabbit hole,
rediscover yourself in Wonderland?
Can you change positions
not travelling through space in between?

Yeah and you want to know what the third key can do?

How many keys do you have?

Only two, but you turn them into as many as you need.
When you turn the third key you do whatever you want in none days
or make whatever you want, anywhere now.

You mean it eliminates time?
Do past, present and future gush all at once?

Yeah.

What else can these keys do?

Mom, I can't tell you everything

Salad

Lured to our garden by the smell of ripe tomatoes
my daughter follows with questions on marriage.
We place some pickings in the basket and cross the path
to greens.   Tearing off a few leaves—our fingers
approach each plant as one might a stranger,
asking permission, expressing
gratitude.   This my daughter knows without asking.

Leaves fall like petals into the basket.
Arugula, butter leaf, radicchio, tat sai, red leaf, romaine.
The plants guide our hands.
Rosemary, oregano, cilantro, parsley, green onion.
Outside, rinsing greens, she returns
worms to soil.
Inside we crush garlic, cover herbs
with oil pressed from the heart of Tuscany and vinegar
aged slowly in flasks of five woods
before joining such fragrance.   This vinegar,
the farmer explained, makes most seem worthy
of washing floors.   Then the peppercorns.
White, green, red, black.   Uncertain
how much to grind, my daughter asks.
She pours this aromatic mixture into a large wooden bowl,
coats it in spirals
bottom to top.

I sharpen the knife to glide through tomatoes.
Float them in liquid gold. Into the bowl
we fluff leaves like feathers.
She catches one
with flecks of earth.
Stops.
Looks through them all again,
returns some to the basin.   Then the grasses.
Buckwheat and sunflower.

My daughter is reminded by my breathing
not to rush.
She is learning how to toss salad
working her fingers
the way she might lift a butterfly
without harming wings.

Now some feta lightly sprinkled. The sprouts.
Adzuki, radish, chickpea, mung, clover.
She decorates the bowl with nasturtiums.
As we set the table her questions roll in with the tide.
Would you tell me more about marriage?

You already know what matters.

How can I?   I'm only a kid.

You touched the plants gently,
blending without sacrifice
the uniqueness of each one's gift.
And you didn't pretend
to know everything
or try to cover your mistakes.

Living on Island

Through the sea of soft tissue I call my body
liquid landscapes pulsing
I sense the heartbeat   this blue planet
the vigorous yes   green
longing itself   toward light.
Here   where rolling water
and upright water   meet
where I   call home.
Here   things of the world   crash
like my own relentless chatter
as waves upon the shore.
For a moment
I disenthrall from the turbulence.
I am
an ocean reconciled
depth to surface.

I am brought into remembering—
waves of time atop the formless.
Brought to freedom
by obedience,
listening choicelessly,
the way monks abide the monastery bell.

Brought here by devotion,
brought here as a parent.
The chimes—
blood insistence of children.
The discipline—
each purpose giving way.

About the Author

Risa Kaparo is a teacher, therapist, author and award-winning poet who makes her home on the island of Kauai. Her poems, articles and essays have appeared in a wide variety of journals, magazines and anthologies. *Embrace* is her first published collection.

Risa grew up in New York City and earned an M.A. in Fiber Arts from Goddard College. She moved to California in 1975 and earned her M.A. and Ph.D. in Counseling Psychology from the Professional School for Psychological Studies.

Her life, like that of the Handless Maiden, was transformed when a life-threatening illness challenged her to grow beyond the conventions of her schooling and learn how to heal herself from the inside out. This eventually led to the birth of her life's work, *Somatic Learning*[sm], a methodology of transformative healing based on a synthesis of psychological, somatic and meditative disciplines.

Risa has taught *Somatic Learning*[sm], at M.I.T., John F. Kennedy University, the California Institute of Integral Studies and numerous other universities and professional institutions. She also teaches creative writing from a *Somatic Learning*[sm] perspective that turns the act of writing into a channel for expressive movement, performance art, self-exploration and renewal.

Risa maintains a private practice in Hawaii and California and gives lectures, seminars and workshops throughout North America, Europe, and Asia.

Also from Scarlet Tanager Books:

Wild One by Lucille Lang Day
poetry, 100 pages, $12.95

*The "Fallen Western Star" Wars: A Debate About
Literary California,* edited by Jack Foley
essays, 85 pages, $14.00

Catching the Bullet & Other Stories by Daniel Hawkes
fiction, 64 pages, $12.95

Visions: Paintings Seen Through the Optic of Poetry
by Marc Elihu Hofstadter
poetry, 72 pages, $14.00

red clay is talking by Naomi Ruth Lowinsky
poetry, 142 pages, $14.95

Everything Irish by Judy Wells
poetry, 112 pages, $12.95

~Reading e Lucy Day's poems
are the feminine the thinking
These are thinking poems
3/24/2002 ~ Bernas Clare

Marc Elihu Hofstadter

The man does what he
calls "prose poems" &
he too tells us of what
his small words contain
— small, almost tiny
subjects

~ Risa is the best reader
a soft suede voice
seduces you to a gushing
flow of words
that have a hundred
...my dim ear, low...
...edges of the words...
...on like I...
...when her voice rises...
...she goes over